Bot Maker

BUILD YOUR OWN RACER BOT

Tucker Besel

BLACK RABBIT BOOKS

Hi Jinx is published by Black Rabbit Books
P.O. Box 227, Mankato, Minnesota, 56002.
www.blackrabbitbooks.com

Jennifer Besel, editor; Michael Sellner, designer;
Omay Ayres, photo researcher

Library of Congress Cataloging-in-Publication Data
Names: Besel, Tucker, author.
Title: Build your own racer bot / by Tucker Besel.
Description: Mankato, Minnesota : Black Rabbit Books, [2018] | Series: Hi jinx. Bot maker | Audience: Age 9-12. | Audience: Grade 4 to 6. | Includes bibliographical references and index.
Identifiers: LCCN 2017009967 | ISBN 9781680723236 (library binding) | ISBN 9781680723533 (e-book) | ISBN 9781680726473 (paperback) |
ISBN 978-1-64466-324-0 (paperback)
Subjects: LCSH: Mobile robots—Design and construction—Juvenile literature.| Robotics—Competitions—Juvenile literature. | Automobiles, Racing—Models—Design and construction—Juvenile literature.
Classification: LCC TJ211.415 .B4733 2018 |
DDC 629.8/932—dc23
LC record available at https://lccn.loc.gov/2017009967

Printed in the United States.

Image Credits

Grant Gould, all robot illustrations
Dreamstime: Simm49, 5 (alligator clip); Newscom: FRANCK ROBICHON, 20 (r); Science Source: NASA, 20 (l); Shutterstock: 7th Son Studio, 5 (connector); Agor2012, Cover, 2-3, 19, 22 (helmet); AlexLMX, 5 (battery); Arcady, 14 (sticker); Art'nLera, 3, 12, 21 (bkgd); Artisticco, 4 (track); belka_35, 5 (scissors); Bill Fehr, 5, 9 (screwdriver); Bplanet, 5 (motor); BW Folsom, 5 (straw); Carolyn Franks, 5 (cardboard); Dualororua, 17 (hands); elbud, 5 (cap); Fedorov Oleksiy, 5 (pencil); Fejas, 1 (flags); Fleur_de_papier, 9 (yellow tape); Galyna G, Cover, Back Cover, 1, 7, 8, 11, 15, 18-19 (grid bkgd); GraphicsRF, 11, 21 (hands); Harish Marnad, Cover, 19, 22 (helmet); hoomoo, 5, 14 (pliers); iceink, 5, 6, 12 (glue gun); Ilya Chalyuk, 3, 4, 6, 20 (marker strokes); Jumnong, 5 (tape); larryrains, 11, 21 (tire); Macrovector, 16 (bkgd); mayakova, 5 (rubber band); Nosopyrik, 5, 7 (ruler); opicobello, Cover (highlighter); Orapin Thepsuttinun, 5 (cardboard); Pasko Maksim, Back Cover, 11, 23, 24 (torn paper); PILart, 6 (splash); Pitju, 3, 13, 21 (curled paper); Pixel Embargo, 7, 10 (pencil); Rohit Dhanaji Shinde, Cover, 2–3, 7, 10, 12, 19, 22, 24 (ant); Rvector, Cover, 19, 22 (flag & steering wheel); S K Chavan, 9 (cone); SeDmi, 5 (skewer); Teguh Mujiono, Cover, 8, 11, 19, 22 (ladybug & firefly); Thomas Bethge, 5 (craft sticks); totallypic, 7, 8-9, 11, 12, 14-15, 16, 18 (arrows); Tueris, 1, 8 (marker); Yayayoyo, 11 (tire face)Every effort has been made to contact copyright holders for material reproduced in this book. Any omissions will be rectified in subsequent printings if notice is given to the publisher.

CONTENTS

Chapter 1

BE A BOT MAKER

Robots aren't just for TV. People make robots that walk, run, and fight. Even beginners can create bots that race.

This book will help you make a simple racing robot. Robot building takes practice. Don't give up if something doesn't work. Experiment until it does. And, most importantly, have fun!

WHAT YOU'LL NEED

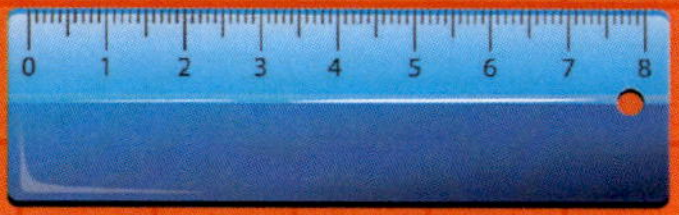

ruler

scissors

electrical tape

sharpened pencil

2 wooden skewers

1 medium-sized rubber band

4 4½-inch- (11-cm-) long wood craft sticks

1¼-inch (3-cm) alligator clip

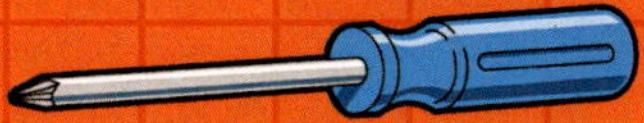
Phillips screwdriver

2 straws

pliers

1 8 x 4-inch (20 x 10-cm) rectangle of corrugated cardboard

hot glue gun and hot glue

9-volt battery

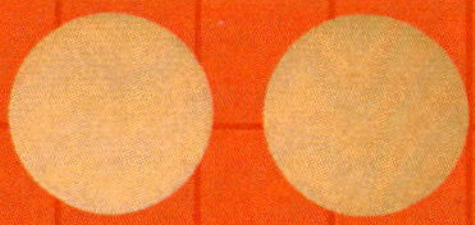
2 ¾-inch- (2-cm-) diameter circles of corrugated cardboard

9-volt battery snap connector (with ½ inch [1 cm] of wire exposed)

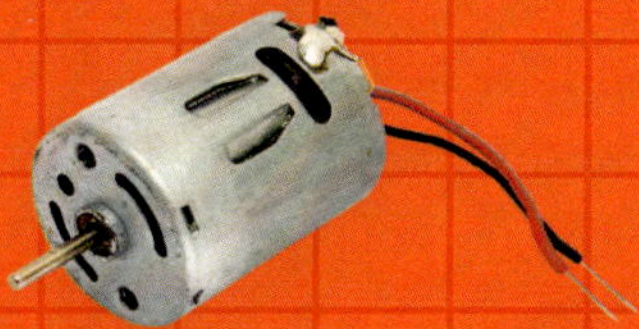
6-volt toy motor with wires (with ½ inch [1 cm] of wire exposed)

2 1-inch- (3-cm-) diameter circles of corrugated cardboard

4 identical soft drink bottle caps

Chapter 2

LET'S BUILD!

1. Hot glue a craft stick along one long side of the cardboard rectangle. Line up the end of the stick with a corner. Repeat with another stick on the other long side.

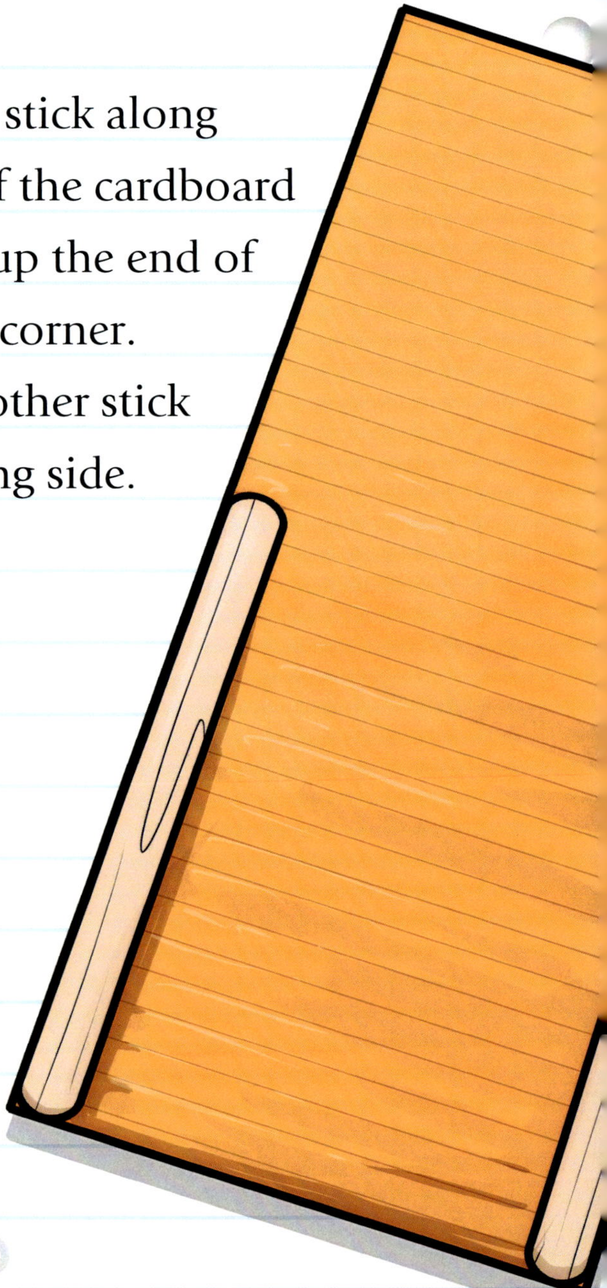

2. Glue two more sticks to the cardboard as shown in the illustration. The short side with the sticks in the corners is the front of the car. Write "front" along this edge.

3. Cut a 4-inch (10-cm) piece from each straw.

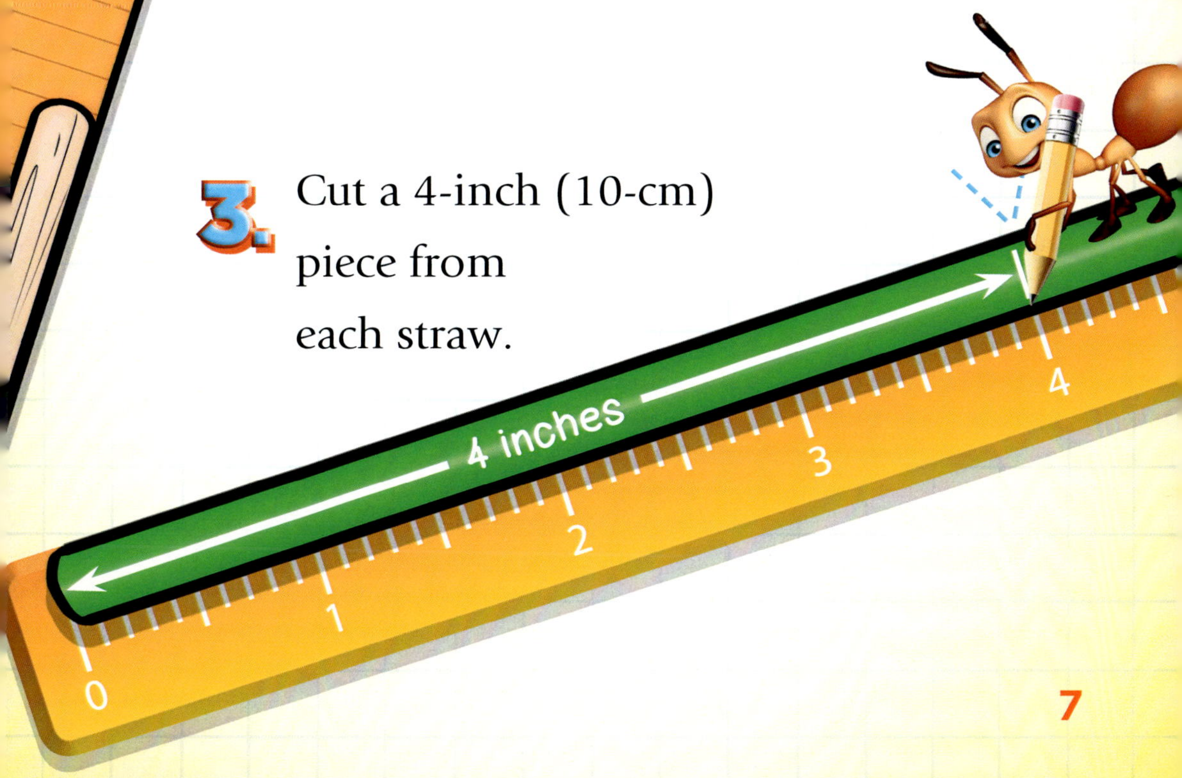

4. Flip the cardboard over. Hot glue a straw piece **parallel** to one short edge. It should be 1 inch (3 cm) from the edge. Repeat with the other straw on the other edge.

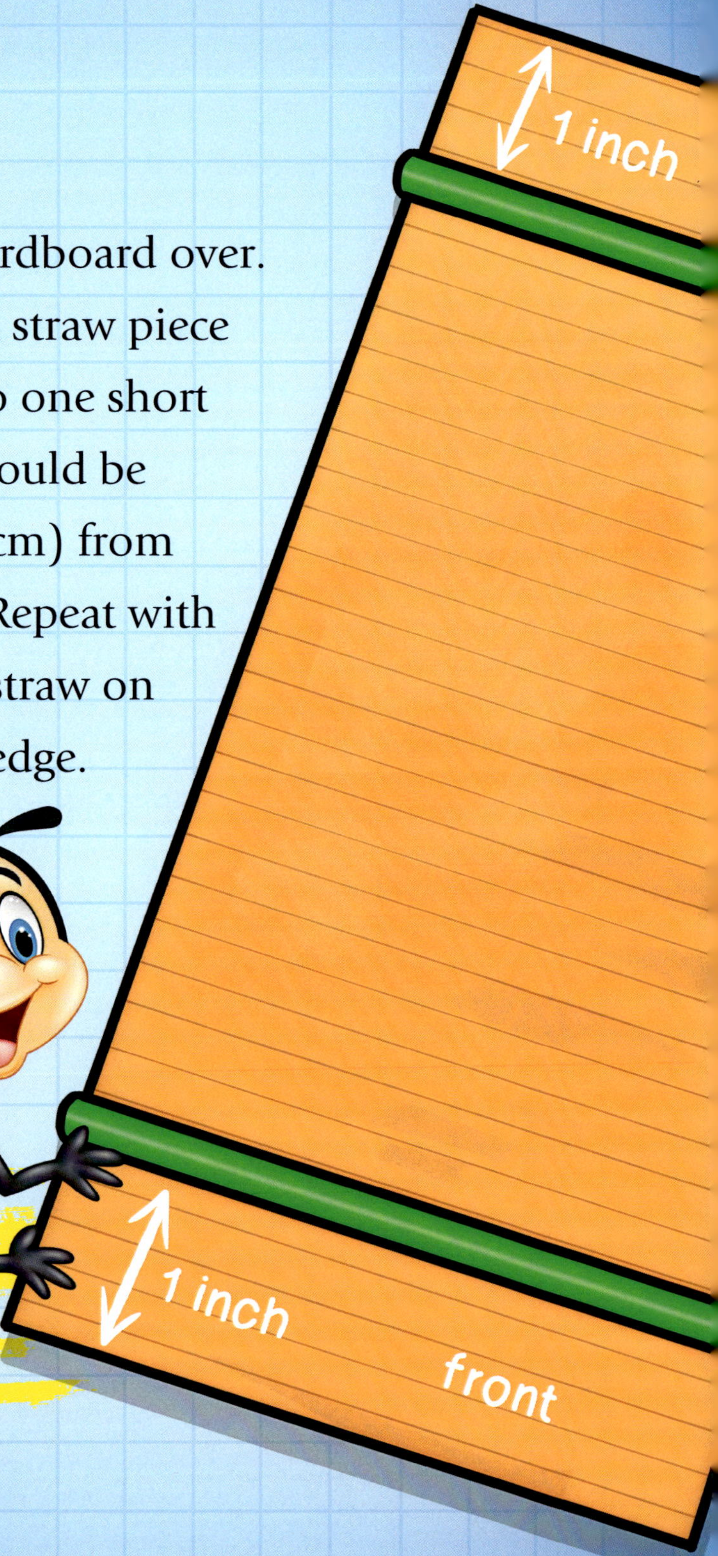

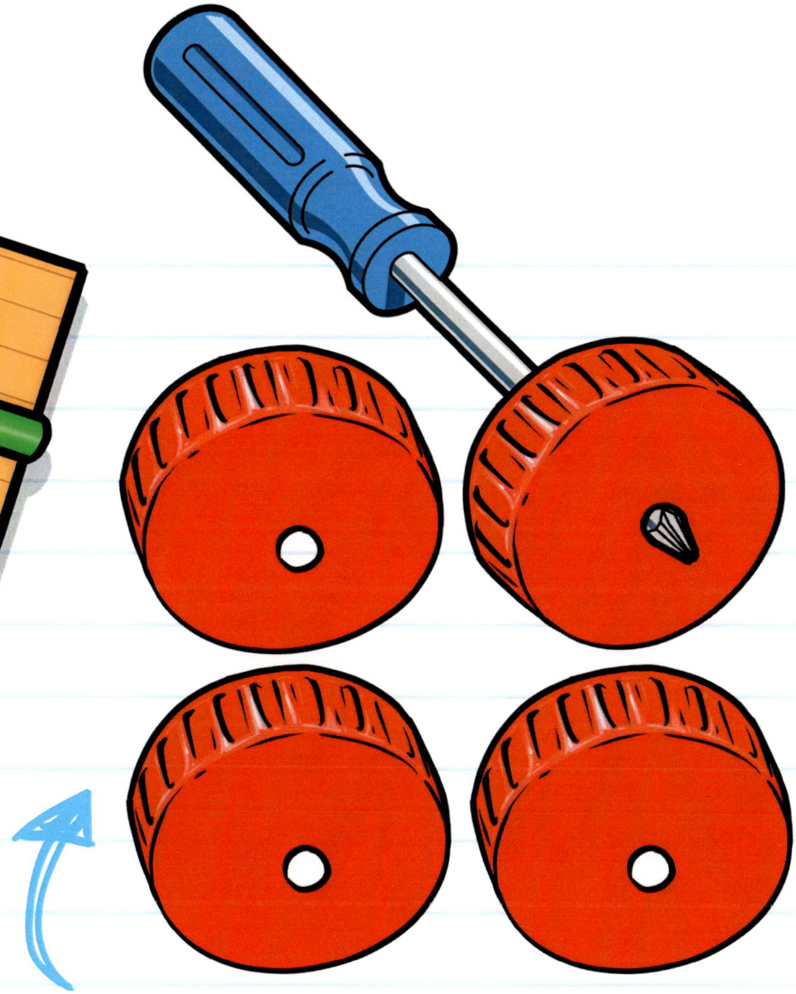

5. Use the screwdriver to poke a hole in the center of each bottle cap.

CAUTION CAUTION CAUTION

Have an adult help you poke the holes.

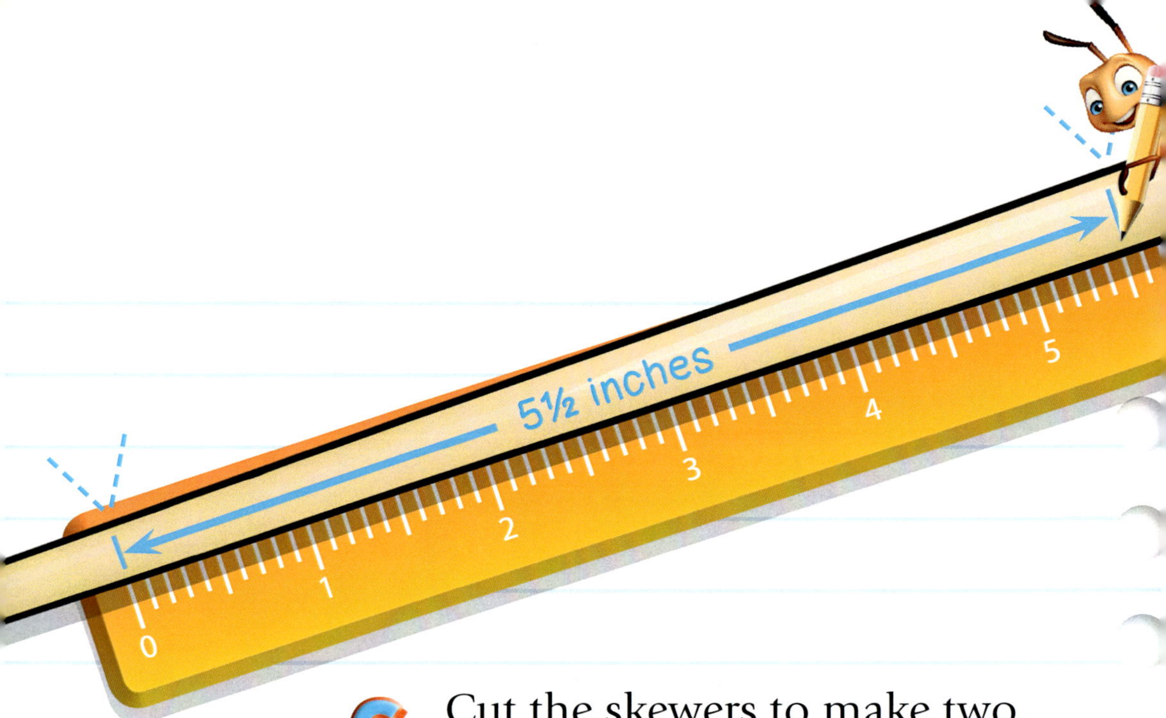

6. Cut the skewers to make two 5½-inch (14-cm) pieces.

7. Slide a bottle cap onto the end of each skewer. Face the top side of the caps out.

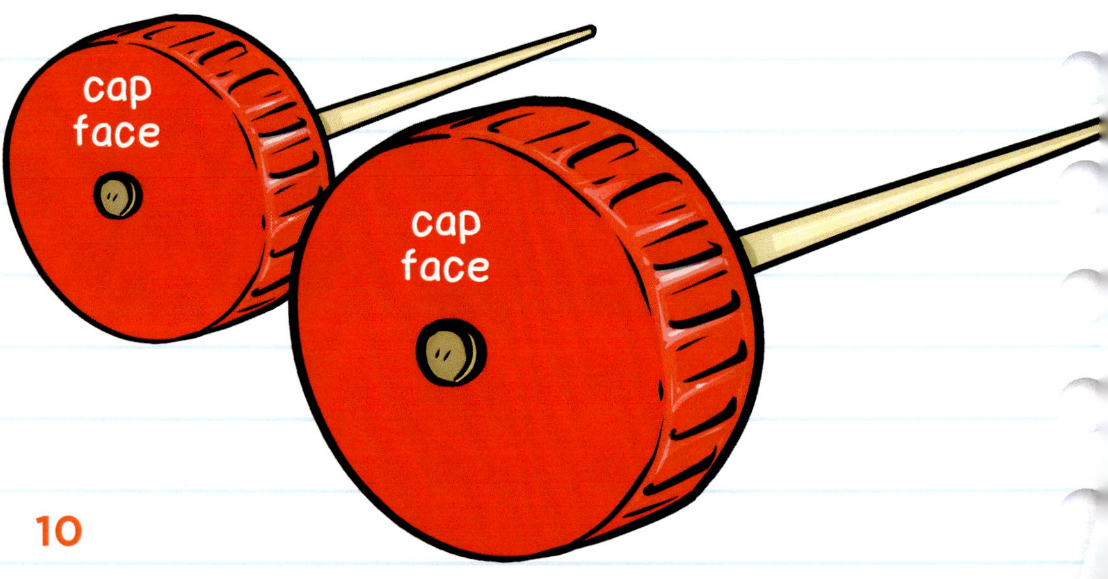

8. Thread one skewer through the front straw. Then slide a cap on the other side of the skewer.

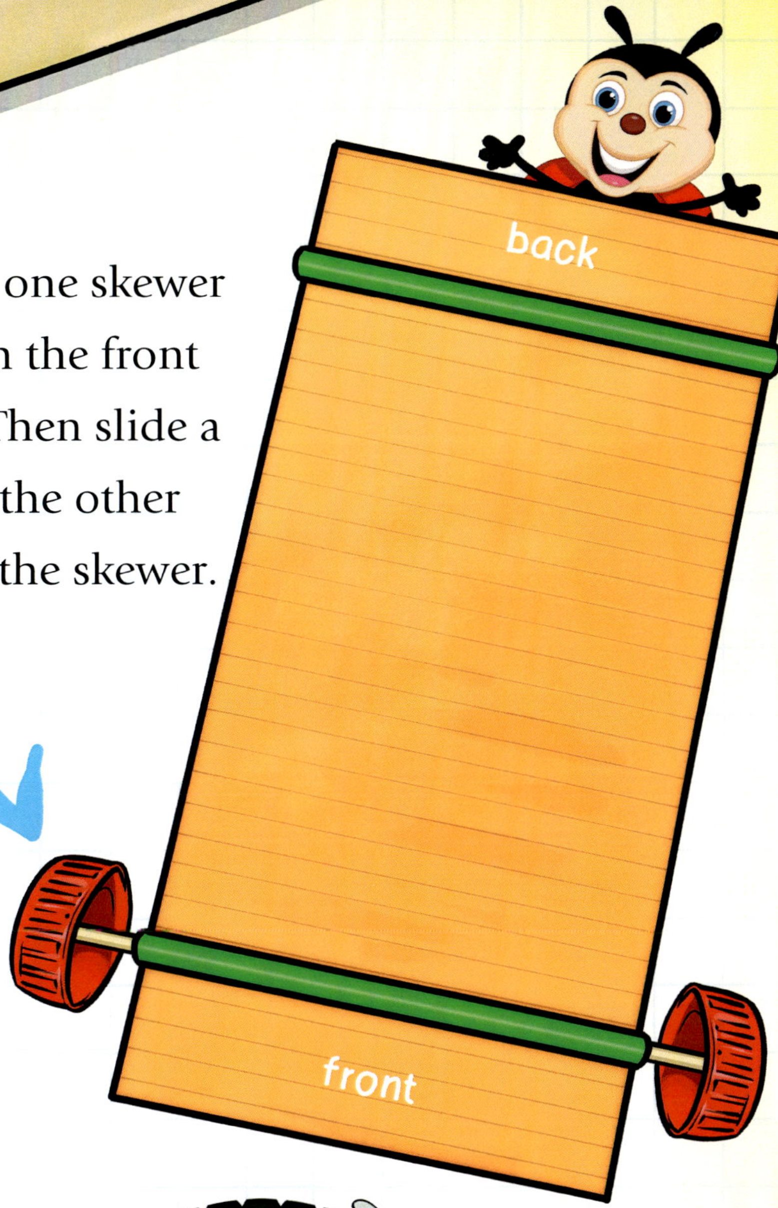

JOKE BREAK

What car part is the laziest?
The wheel ... because it's always tired!

9. Poke center holes through each cardboard circle. A skewer tip works well for this.

10. Sandwich one small circle between the two larger circles. Line up the holes. Hot glue them together.

11. Slide the circle sandwich onto the other skewer from step 7. Put the circles close to, but not inside, the cap. Hot glue the circles in place.

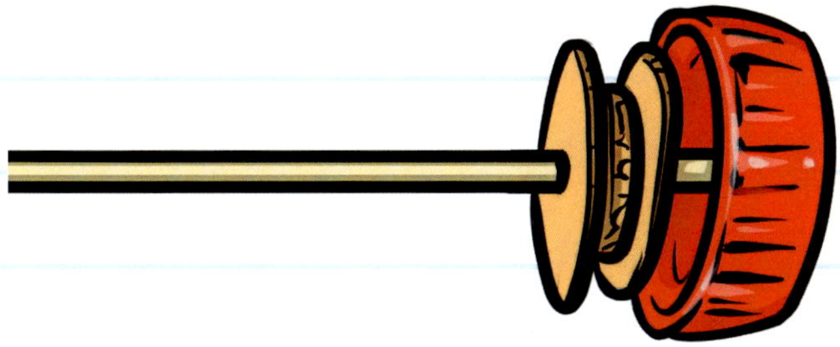

12. Slide the skewer through the back straw. Put the last bottle cap on the other end of the skewer.

13. Hot glue the tips of each skewer to the caps. You don't want the wheels to fall off!

14. Attach the alligator clip to the red wire from the motor. To do this, put the wire between the tabs on the back of the clip. Then use pliers to pinch the tabs together.

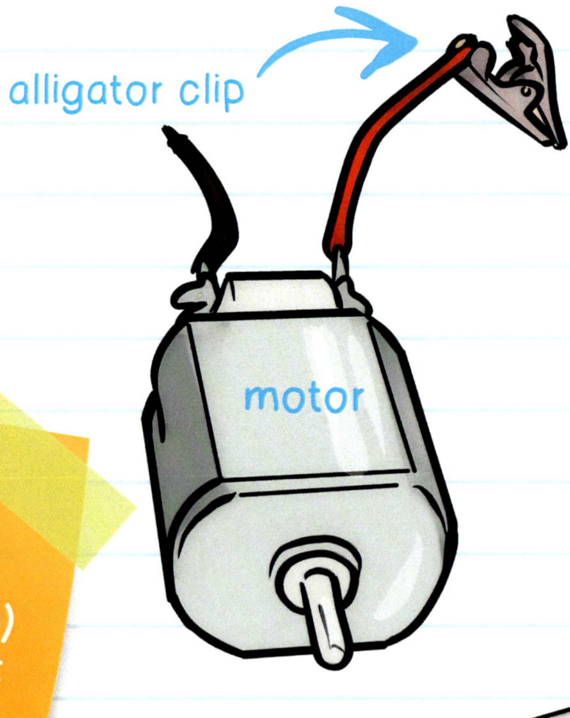

The record for fastest car is 763 miles (1,228 km) per hour. Your robot racer will not go that fast.

15. Connect the black wires from the battery connector and the motor. Hold the exposed parts of the black wires side by side. Then twist the exposed ends together. Snap a battery into the connector. **Clamp** the alligator clip to the connector's exposed red wire. The motor's **shaft** should spin. Unclamp the clip.

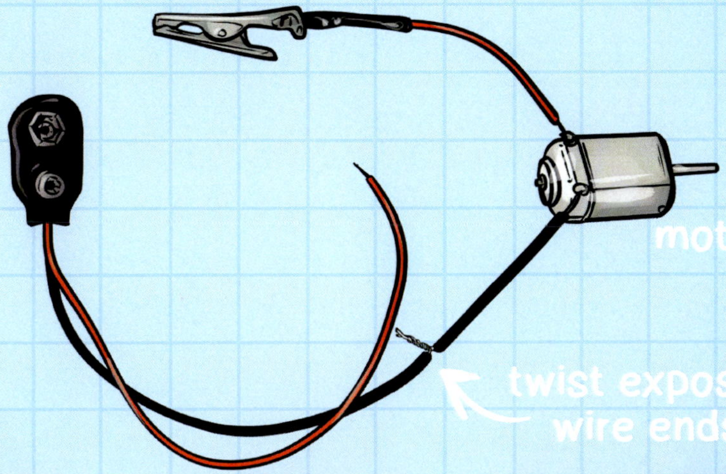

battery in connector

shaft

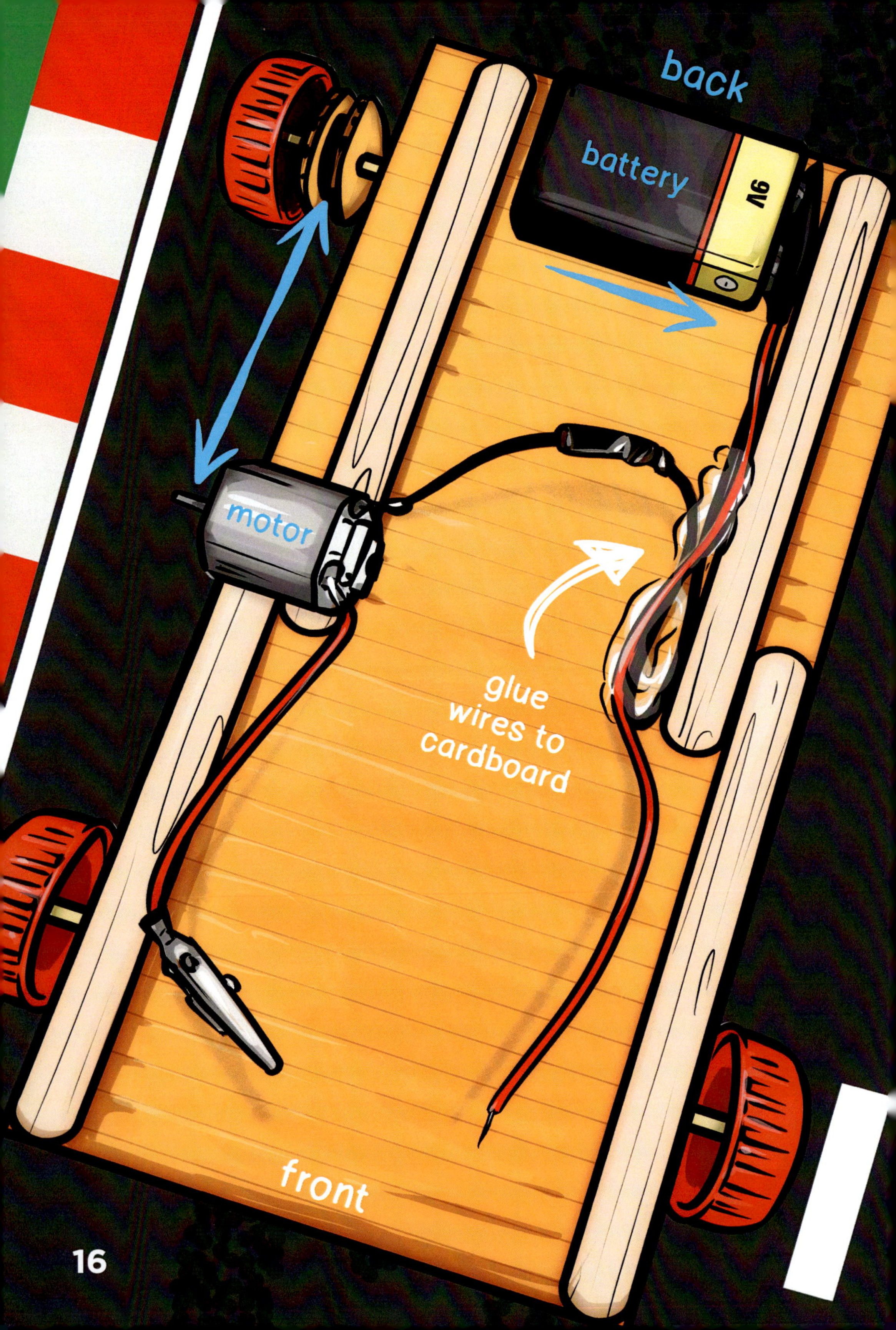
back
battery
9V
motor
glue wires to cardboard
front

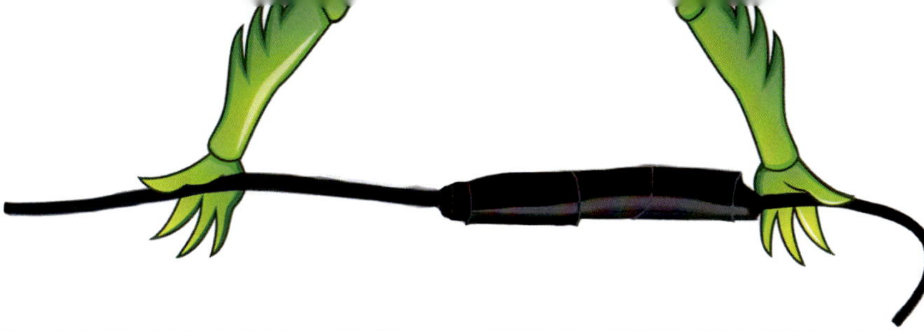

16. Bend the twisted wire ends down. Wrap them to the black wire with electrical tape.

17. Flip the car over. Glue the battery along the back edge of the cardboard body. Face the wires away from the cardboard circles.

18. Glue the motor to the craft sticks, where they **overlap**. The motor's shaft should line up with the cardboard circles.

19. Clean up the wires. Fold them together, and hot glue them to the cardboard. Make sure the alligator clip reaches the exposed red wire.

20. Slide the last cardboard circle onto the motor's shaft. Hot glue the circle in place.

21. Put the rubber band on the motor's shaft. Then loop it over the circle sandwich. It should rest on the small circle.

22. Clamp the alligator clip to the exposed wire. Watch your racer robot rush off!

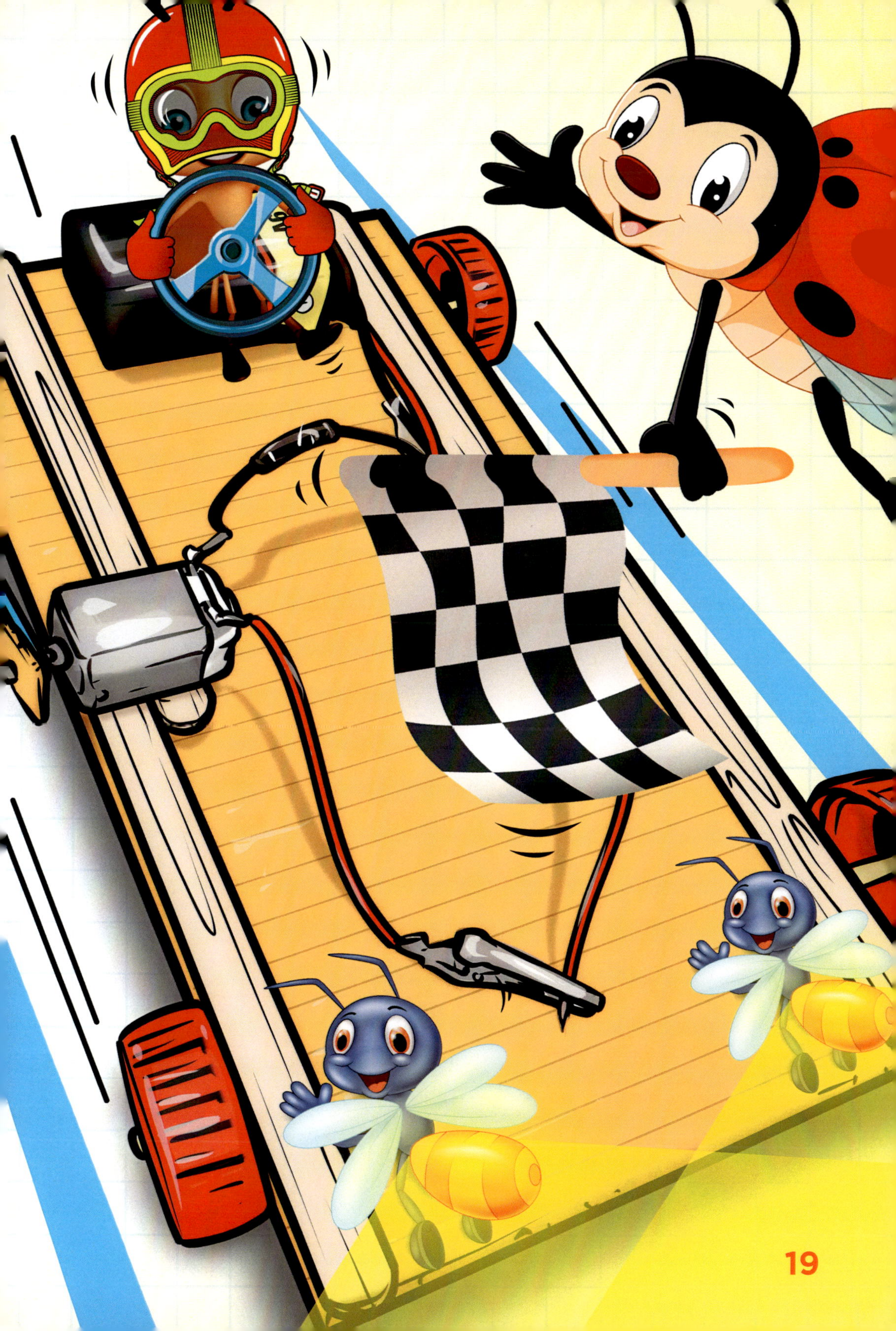

Chapter 3
GET IN ON THE HI JINX

Scientists use the same basic skills you did to build robots. Medical robots save lives. Space robots explore planets. Now you have basic robot-building skills. How will you change the world?

Take It One Step More

1. What other materials could you use for the body?

2. Why are the wood craft sticks needed?

3. How could you build on this design? Is there a way to make this robot start and stop on its own?

GLOSSARY

clamp (KLAMP)—to hold tightly

diameter (dy-AH-muh-tur)—the length of a straight line through the center of an object

exposed (ek-SPOZD)—not covered

overlap (oh-vur-LAP)—to extend over or past

parallel (PEHR-uh-lel)—extending in the same direction and not meeting

shaft (SHAFT)—a cylindrical bar used to support rotating pieces

LEARN MORE

BOOKS

Ceceri, Kathy. *Making Simple Robots.* Sebastopol, CA: Maker Media, 2015.

Kopp, Megan. *Maker Projects for Kids Who Love Electronics.* Be a Maker! New York: Crabtree Publishing Company, 2017.

McCombs, Kevin. *Locomotion and Mechanics.* Robotics. New York: Cavendish Square Publishing, 2017.

WEBSITES

All about Robots
www.kidsdiscover.com/teacherresources/all-about-robots/

Build Your First Robot
www.popularmechanics.com/technology/robots/a7388/build-your-first-robot/

History of Robotics: Timeline
www.robotshop.com/media/files/PDF/timeline.pdf

TIPS AND TRICKS

Adults are boring. But they can be really helpful. Don't be afraid to ask for help if you get stuck.

If your wires don't have exposed ends, don't worry. Use a wire stripper to take off as much of the wire casing as needed. (See first tip.)

If the wheels keep spinning out, try putting lines of hot glue on the wheels.

The author is super cool. He made a short video of his racer bot. Check it out on Black Rabbit Books' YouTube channel.